T0365370

Chasing Mirages

Jack Duke

Print information available on the last page

Book Designer: Jonah Goodman
Art Director: Mike Nardone

Rev. date: 10/16/2019

To order additional copies of this book, contact:
Xlibris
1-888-795-4274
www.Xlibris.com
Orders@Xlibris.com

At the tip of the peninsula stood a solitary tree,
Which, by virtue of its aloneness,
grew to the fullest-fed grace its
heritage would allow.

My mind melts.

Its guards, lulled by sound,

Lie down.

Unknown words appear,

Silently, bashfully,

Growing, daring, dancing

Between the puddles.

My pen thinks.

I live.

All that I am is less than it seems
For I'm really reducible to chemicals.
I think, I feel, I dream, I love…
Yet, there is no me,
For I am a figment of my own imagination.
It's easier to understand
If you think of me as a horse.
Isn't it preposterous to think of a horse
Wanting to be a rabbit, or a king, or a saint?
And how ridiculous that a horse
Could ever want to write a poem,
Or sit and think by mixing up brain chemicals.
There's nothing inside a horse's bony skull
But an electric brain, governed by chemicals.
"Fix 'em up, send 'em back to the plow.
Ain't got no business bein' anything but a horse."
Christ called us sheep.
It's all the same.
Two bony skulls pretending to talk.
Love, Hate, Fear…all chemicals in flesh
Made out of dirt.
Three brains am I, two old, one new,
And all the madness of the universe
Lives inside my head.

I am the spirit of the rock,
The shattered, scattered sound
Of the moment that all began;
A shred of melody
Shot into the emptiness of forever.
Ohhh, how I hated the sun!
Burn and freeze, here and gone,
Wishy-washy sun.
But I loved the rain.
With the patience of eternity
It bathed away the layers
Of my tomb, and I escaped
To seek an eternity of life.

                              The planets of my mind
Whirl their paths

                                                                    Through sanity

        And madness;
                Sometimes aligned   Sometimes
        In the disarray of ordered randomness;
                                From hate through hope
                        Love through despair
                            In cycled rhythms
                            Of natural time,

        They go
From A to B
                Then B to C

                                        Then A to C

For A is death
                B is life

                                    And C is
                The victory of creation.

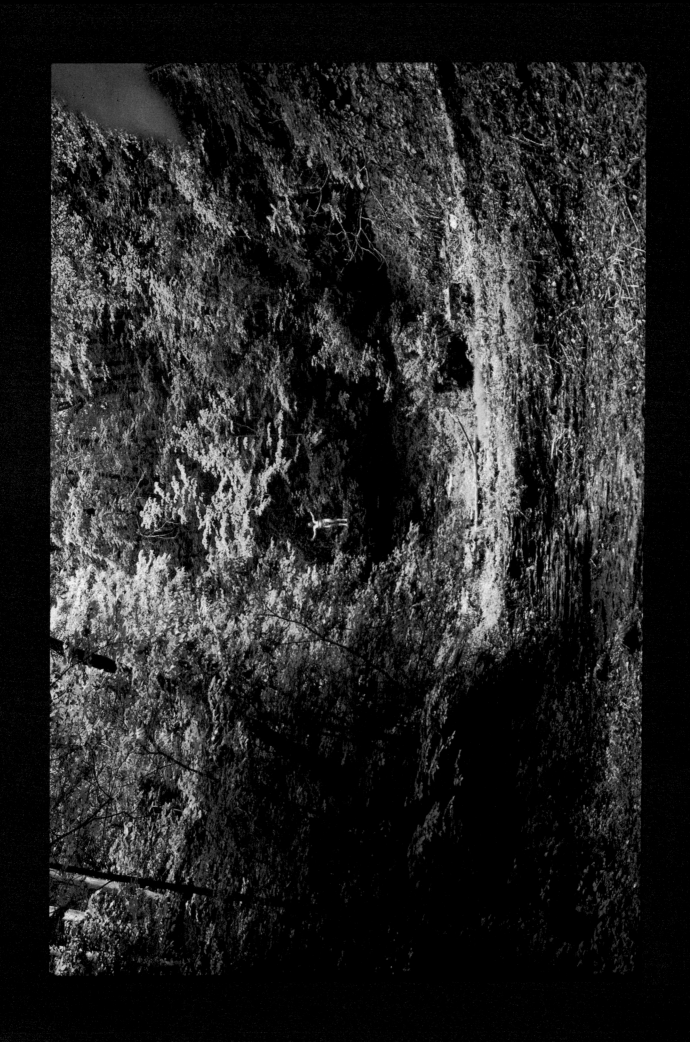

Behind me lies a trail of ragged clothes...
Diapers
I didn't know I wore, nor why;
Underwear
Yellowed by a stubbed toe that made me pee my pants;
Torn hand-me-downs
Stained from wrestling in the grass;
Shiny-black dress pants
With tattle-tale traces on the fly;
Faded fatigues
Aching with military fitness;
The Sears-Roebuck suit of a new father;
A row of business suits
In ever-increasing sizes;
A hospital gown
Wretched with vomit,
Lying in the castaway lane
Unfit for rags.
Behind me lies a trail of ragged clothes...
Today
I am naked in the sun.

The unspent energy of her denials
Found the poles of my loneliness
And the storm was joined.
We shed our substance in furious thunder,
As if our wills controlled the storm,
And scorched our souls with zigzagging orgasms
That stripped away ignorance
And rumbled through emptiness
With expectations of love without horizons.

But, now, the storm has passed.
The rain falls gently as tears.
The wind that drove us
Lies quietly on the water.
Did one of us enter the river
And the other find the earth?
Tomorrow's sun will show me truth.
Then I shall search for flowers
And throw a bouquet
On the passing waters.

With linked arms and sober glasses,
We courted with ancient rite an ancient dream
And agreed to love.
A wishing pond caught our coins
And joined our hopes to a thousand others
Who sought to shape time, itself,
To lovers' wills.
Above a Kirlian camera, our fingertips touched,
Then our lips, and branded our auras
Into the library of our dreams.
The shower that tattooed her breasts
Flowed through my throat into the forests of my mind
And turned them green again.
When we sat in a bath of overflowing laughter,
All the oceans of the world had no greater call
Nor mysteries to explore.
Then, dancing to the music of a blind TV,
Our nudeness glided by on a looking glass.
Perfection was buried in gentle awkwardness,
But what was reflected was real,
And what was real,
I loved.

Donna Marie, free spirit.

Whatever her name,

It separates her from all other humans.

It makes her communion with God,

Nature, and her own nature

A reality known to none but her.

It is the secret that cannot be shared,

The responsibility that cannot be shirked,

The power that cannot be defeated.

It is the original miracle of creation,

The beginning of the dream of love,

A part of the end of everything.

It is a butterfly and a bowling ball,

A sword and a broom,

A book and a dream.

It is the purification

The annointment

And the blessing.

Donna Marie.

I loved Donna Marie.

Ten million years you've roamed this earth,
Six million more than man.
You saw the world when it was new,
Before man's reign began.
Your claws tore flesh
And your fangs dripped blood
As you did what was meant to be done;
God gave you your share of daily bread,
But always, it had to be won.
Then into the Eden of man you came,
Where you no longer had to kill
But were free to relax and explore your mind,
Your innermost feline will.
Do cats have a Christ?
Were you saved before man?
Is that why you lie there and purr?
Safe in the arms of a loving god,
Yet still, you must kill
The last bird

Like a roller coaster that never stops,
Like a Ferris wheel whose speed of spin
Flings me outward and traps me by my own weight,
Like bumper cars driven by happy idiots
Who crack the bounds and smash into my mind,
Like balloons stretching out to engulf me
Until I dare not throw a dart
Lest I be caught in the explosion.
Like targets throwing bullets back
To beat against my head from my own aimed accuracy,
Like arms snaking out from shadowy sideshows
To degrade me with their ugly truths...
But I must play the games
And take the rides
And see the sights.
Outside the Park
It is dark.

I ride on wings of thought,
Swooping from idea to idea,
Zooming to where my mind
Has never been,
Stalling into blacknesses
That sear me with fear
And make me pray
For the existence of a caring God.

Hither and yon, I fly,
Landing on mountain tops,
Flitting through forests
In outer space,
Challenging madness,
Daring the destruction
Of all that is
So that everything different
Might be loved.

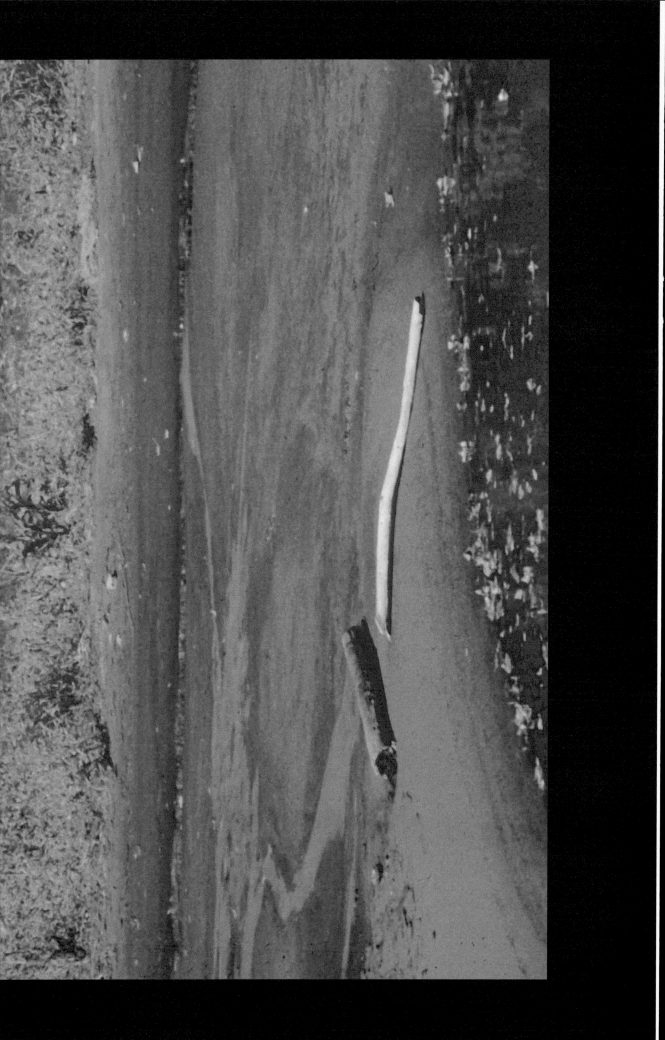

Sometimes I envy people

Who don't know how to think.

They lead such uncomplicated lives.

But even thinkers often lack

The courage to follow their minds.

To think is to create.

To create is to put something new

Where nothing has ever been before.

Scary space can be created

And filled with scary creations

All as real as anything else.

From the darkness of the mind

Come the raw materials of life.

Once in awhile, there is a glint of gold

In the overburden, and one is glad

One is alive. For thinkers,

That is enough.

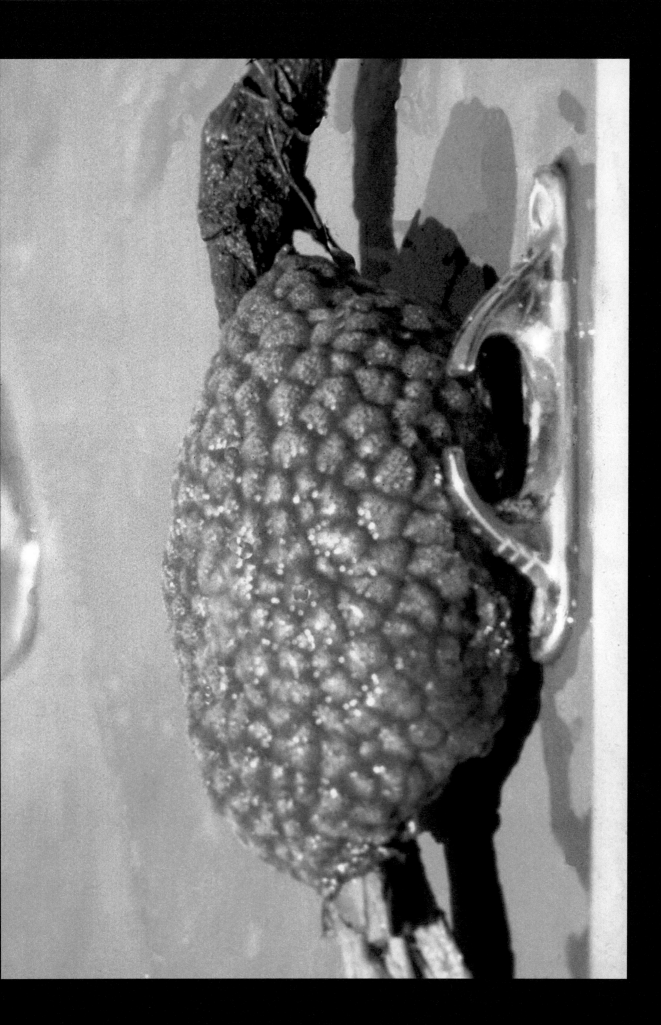

From Darkness of earth
And silence of egg
Come puffs of energy
Wrapped in shells of stardust.

Each moves, each grows,
Each drinks the sun.
Each sends a pulse of power
Into tomorrow, past yesterday's stars
Perfectly reproducing their wonders forever.

I, too, eat the sun,
But add despair of living
And rapture of life
To the trembling truths
I join to the silent stream.

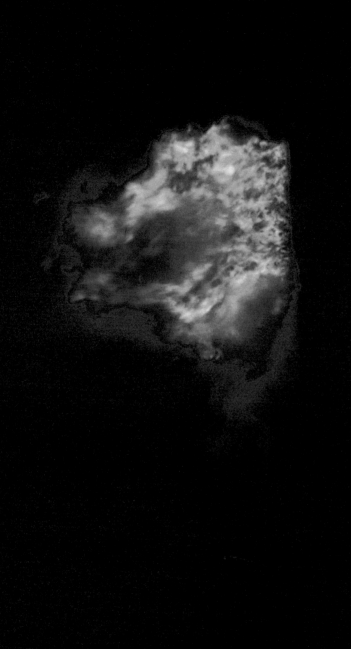

How like a campfire I am;

Leaping and dancing,

Swelling and falling;

Bringing warmth and comfort,

Yet burning those who abuse me;

Flaring out of control,

Yet dimming or dying for lack of fuel;

Destroying and liberating with the same lick.

Though I cannot be embraced,

I bring pleasure to those who surround me

And am dependent on their care

For my very life.

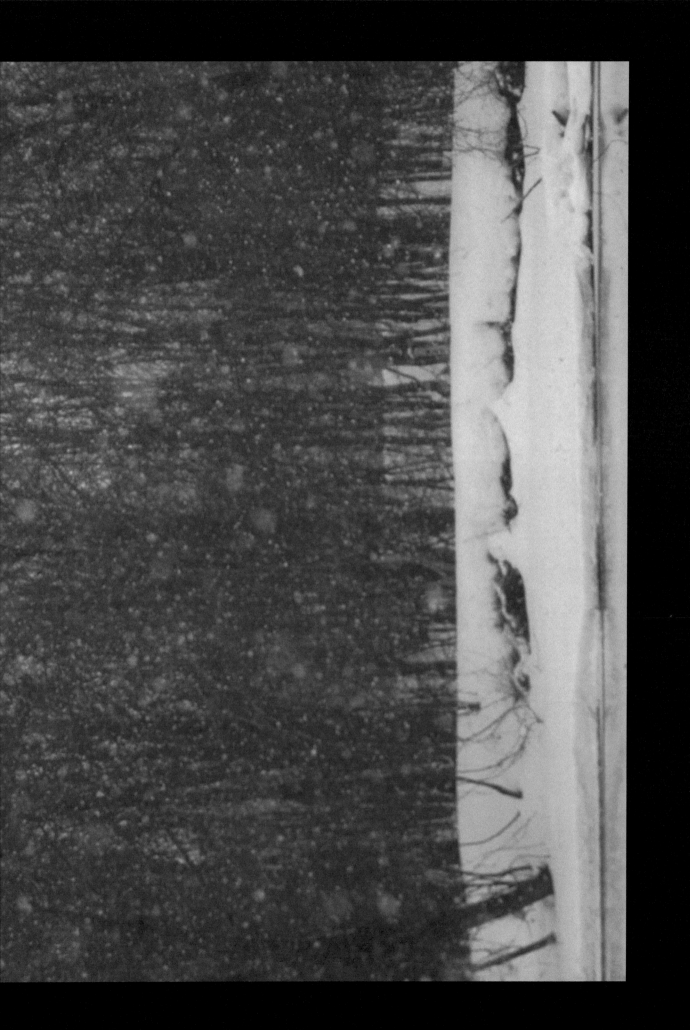

I saw your beauty in November:
Great silent flakes of snow
That hid the dying earth
And blurred the lifeless trees.
Your white replaced the butterfly
And soundless majesty
The noise of Nature's children,
But now, it's March.

In windless skies, you pour
From pregnant clouds
To smother-cover all you find
As if the sun will never
Come again to end your reign.
Where is your beauty now?
I see with my own eyes
What gave them joy
When first you came.
The flakes are just the same.

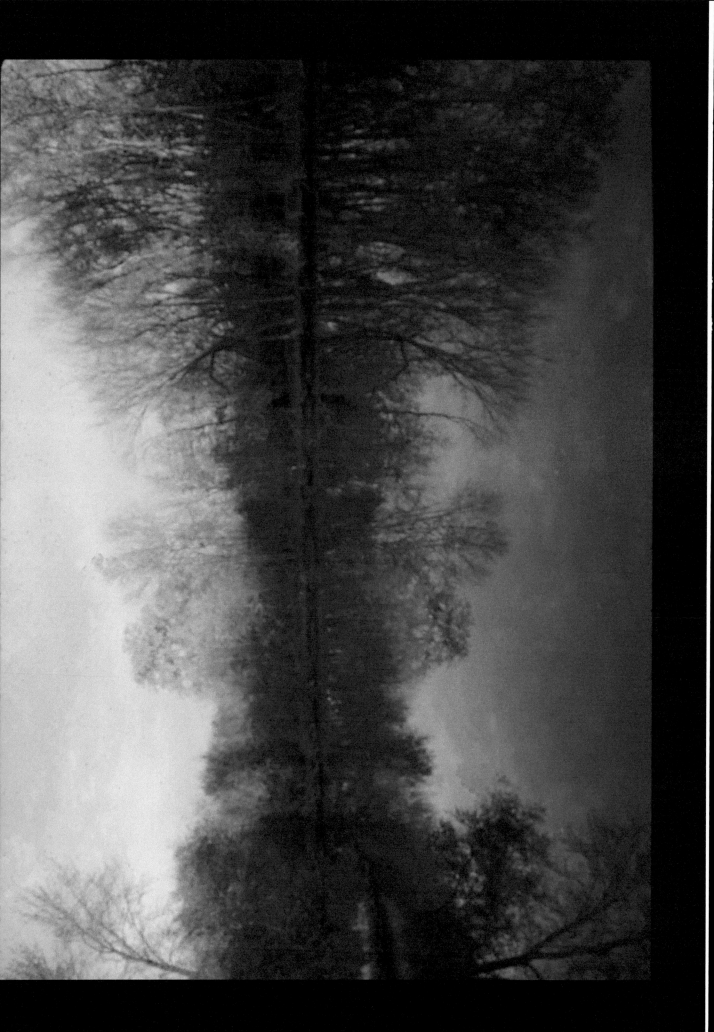

When you are my friend, my sharing friend
I will take you deep
Into the serenity of my wilderness.
I will let you hear the prayer I sing
To the God of Beauty around us.
When we leave, I will show you a mouse
Hanging from a hawk's claws
And tell you of how I exult
In its back-and-forth flight of victory
As if I were to share in the prize.
Then I will show you my tear for the mouse
And I will let you hear
My scream of anger at the God of Cruelty
After, perhaps, we can be silent together
And try to understand.

I wanted patience and was given

A beach of sand to assemble into a mountain;

Courage and was faced

With a decision to change my entire life;

Hope and was forced

Into unceasing despair;

Trust and was handed

A lover with a shadowy past;

Happiness and was offered

The weak, the weary, the confused as friends;

Strength and was loaded

With burdens that rightfully belonged to others;

Peace and was introduced to

The meanings of forever.

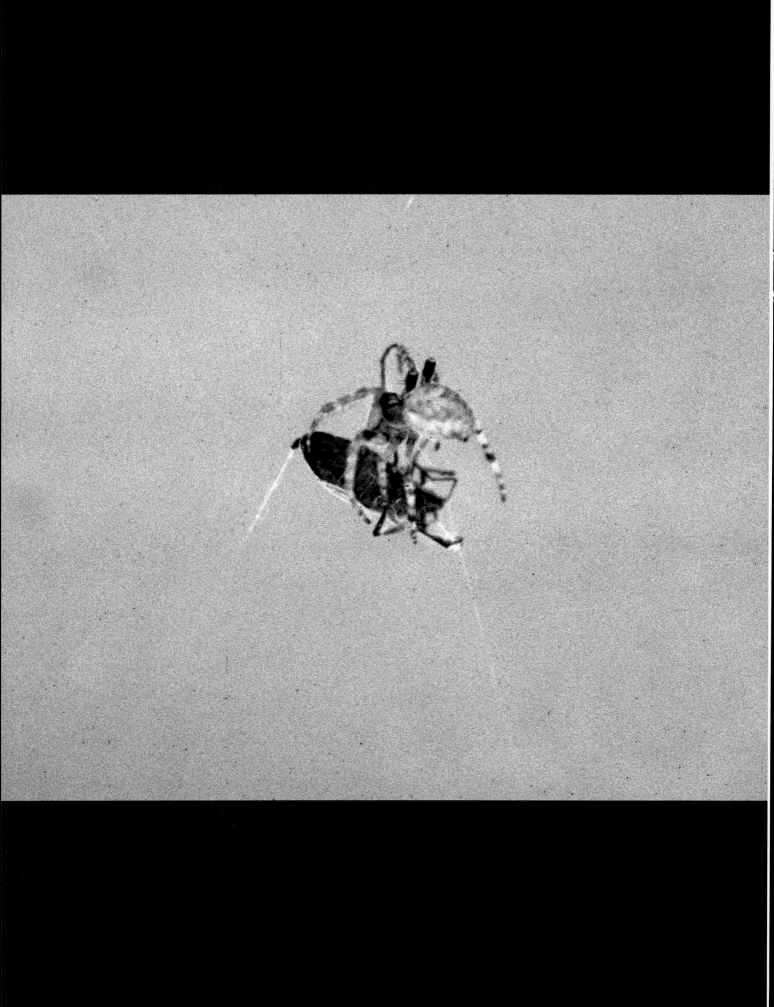

He flew through the air like a red-and-black watermelon seed,
Smashed into a spider's web and watched his life pass in review.
"Why am I locked up in this ridiculous shell?
Granted, it's nice when I fall off a table,
But most of the time, it's just in the way."
His six legs drove their way into deeper desperation
Until only whirring wings could set him free,
But he does not fly. Stupid, stupid bug.
"I banged into my mate in mid-air, too.
It's a wonder she ever let me fertilize her eggs.
That damn spider! She thinks she can hurt me
By pounding on my shell. I'm glad I've got it now."
She rushes atop him. Eight barbed legs clamp his wings
Tightly against his shell. She is fat from a prosperous summer.
"God. Thousands of our kids have already died.
But at least a few dozen of them turned out OK."
She pumps her swollen body in primitive passion,
Drilling through his armor.
"Ouch! She bit a hole right through my neck.
I knew I shouldn't have flown today."
Through hypodermic fangs, the poison starts to ooze.
His legs stir weakly now, ever more weakly.
"I should have stayed at home and made more babies.
Naw. She's too old. Too late now, anyway.
Damned spider's got me tied up so I can't move a claw."

Was it nice to be a box-elder bug?
I'm glad you lived. I'm glad you ate,
And breathed, and bred. And, I hope,
You sang a song that only bugs can understand.
And, when the spider tried to make your life her own,
I hope she failed. I hope something got away.
And I hope it was better to be a box-elder bug
Than not to be at all.

Loving is a gentle strength.

Like the silk of parachute spiders,

It carries beings to lands of new survival.

Then, like the spiders themselves,

Become threads of life

Connecting yesterdays with tomorrows,

Able to foster themselves in

And nourish themselves for

But a tiny quiver of time,

Yet enriching the universe

By simply being.

If I wanted to,
I could make the clouds pink.
I could turn dandelions into blessings
And thank the thornbush for protecting the rabbit.
I could touch the earth with my tongue.
I could run naked and laughing into a thunderstorm
And perch on the edge of a never-ending sunset.
I could make the snow warm.
I could make sense of the death of a deer
And throw away the eye that saw a fault in a friend.
I could hug a rainbow, caress a mushroom,
And waltz on the waves of the wind.
I could make a feeling last forever.
If I wanted to,
I could.

I stole a mother today.

I took her right out of the mouth

Of a friend who didn't want her.

I only know her shadow,

But, on gray-minded days,

She cheers me.

I know she would smile

If she knew of my happy times.

She's a lot better mother

Than my friend remembers.

If I knew where she lived,

I would send her a talking flower.

All it would say is

"Thank you, mom."

When I consider a happy baby in a crib of devotion,
Loved by child and adult, man and woman, stranger and friend,
Called a little angel, that was me in that crib.
A miracle, a gift from God, that was me.
It's still me.
Oh, Lord, keep me humble.

When I am awakened to the beauty
Of our own miraculous assemblages of atoms metamorphosed
Into Life
And find it incomprehensible as to why I'm so fortunate
To be alive, I tremble into ecstasy.
I am alive.
Oh, Lord, keep me humble.

I note that this shell I'm wearing
Protects and defends itself on cellular levels
And my heart shrinks in fear of the holy wars going on
Inside my body.
All for the benefit of me, the inhabitant of this body.
Oh, Lord, keep me humble.

I'm part of the universe. I come from stardust.
My molecules come from the substance of the earth,
My energy, from the sun.
All I have to do, while I'm in my atomic shell,
Is think and feel and explore the partially revealed
Reality of Eternity. I will live forever.
Oh, Lord, keep me humble.

I have no choice about some of the things in my life.
I must feel pain. I must laugh and cry.
I have to love and ponder.
I have to feel good feelings and bad.
There is no choice. There is a perfect God.
Our experience of Life is a part of His reality.
Oh, Lord, keep me humble.

I have been given a spirit that is uniquely mine.
It will live forever. I can shape it any way I want.
It's mine forever and ever.
I look at your spirit to see my own.
Oh Lord, keep me humble.

We are creatures, reaching back forever on a nine-month loom,
Allowed to participate in our own evolution.
That puts a bit of the power of God into us.
We also shape each other, like it or not, forever.
Oh, Lord, keep me humble.

The sun is on the other side of the earth now,
Quiet darkness is my friend
Still...I miss the warmth

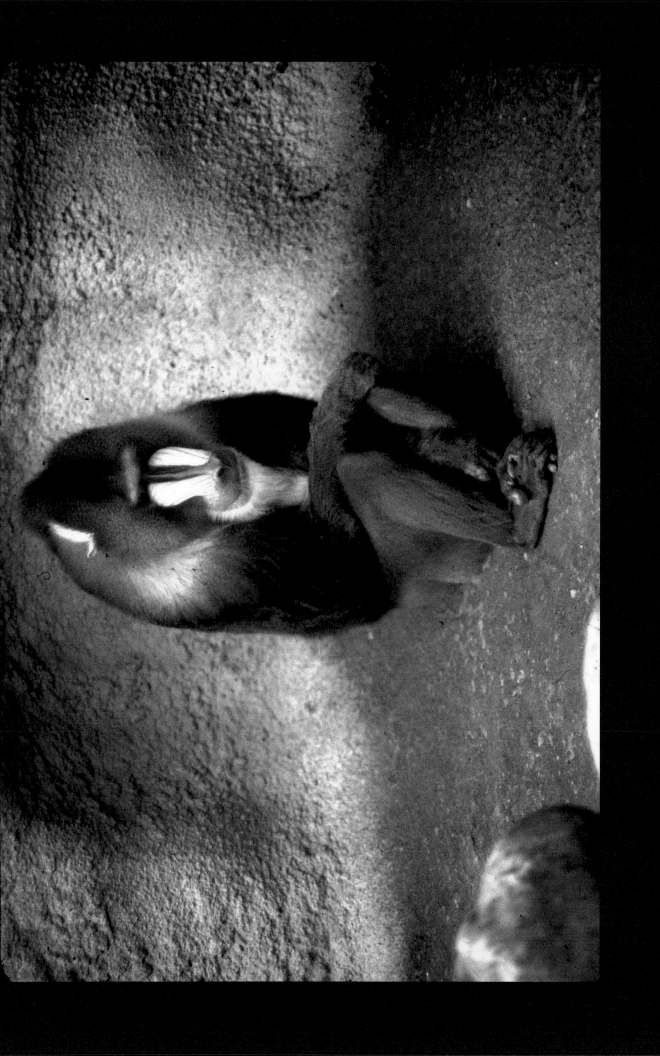

Look out to the edge of the universe

And see the beginning of time.

You cannot look in the other direction,

There is an impregnable line.

The moment of now is the act of creation,

Forever forbidden from sight.

What happens now

is always was,

Though it speeds with

the speed of light

Look out to the edge

of the universe.

There, from the

beginning of time

Infinity flowed

In a single direction

And so did the growth

Of our mind.

Why do you suppose that flowers

Take so long to bloom?

If I were in charge,

I'd make them grow today

And bloom tomorrow.

There'd be a lot more flowers that way,

But some would only see the sun

And others just the gray.

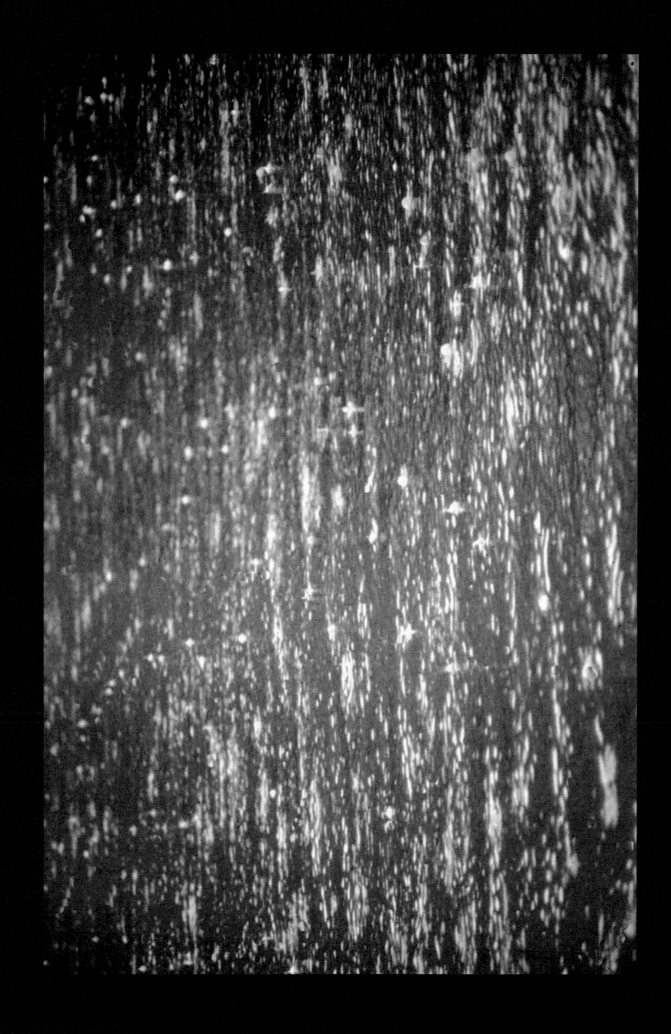

We lazed in the haymow of a weathered old barn
While a thunderstorm came hurrying by.
The rain rapped the tin roof with nerve-resting rhythm
In counterpoint to thunderfilled sky.
Drops bubbled a puddle with high-rising domes
That burst when skittered by winds
Which stole the aroma from fresh-cut alfalfa
And wrapped it around our bare skins.
I reached out to touch her and gather together
The shared joy of being alive.
I found her approaching, as natural as summer,
With happiness sparkling her eyes.
We laid down together like two trusting children
As the shower raced on its own way,
And created a memory as lasting as sunlight
On our country-fresh midsummer's day.

Printed in the United States
By Bookmasters